Sports Illustrated

TIGER WOODS
The Making Of a Champion

Stories excerpted from the pages of *Sports Illustrated*
Original text by John Garrity

SIMON & SCHUSTER

SIMON & SCHUSTER
Rockefeller Center
1230 Avenue of the Americas
New York, NY 10020

Tiger Woods: The Making of a Champion was
produced by Bishop Books Inc., New York City.
Designed by Barbara Chilenskas.

Manufactured in the United States of America

10 9 8 7 6 5 4 3 2 1

Library of Congress Cataloging-in-Publication
Data is available.

Cover photograph: Jacqueline Duvoisin
Back cover photograph: Bob Martin

ISBN: 0-684-84226-2

CONTENTS

4/ **Introduction**
by John Garrity

10/ **Act I: The Kid**
Overview *by John Garrity*
March 9, 1992 **"You the Kid!"** *by John Garrity* /16
August 9, 1993 **No Holding This Tiger** *by John Garrity* /20
September 5, 1994 **The Comeback Kid** *by Tim Rosaforte* /22
October 17, 1994 **Tale of a Tiger** *by Jaime Diaz* /26

28/ **Act II: The Amateur**
Overview *by John Garrity*
March 27, 1995 **Goodness Gracious, He's a Great Ball of Fire** *by Rick Reilly* /34
April 17, 1995 **Out of Sight** *by Jaime Diaz* /42
July 17, 1995 **Out of the Woods** *by Jaime Diaz* /48
September 4, 1995 **Encore! Encore!** *by Tim Rosaforte* /50
April 8, 1996 **A Fast Study** *by Jaime Diaz* /52
June 10, 1996 **In His Sights** *by William F. Reed* /56
June 24, 1996 **What Now?** *by Michael Bamberger* /60

64/ **Act III: The Pro**
Overview *by John Garrity*
September 2, 1996 **Roaring Ahead** *by Jaime Diaz* /70
September 9, 1996 **On the Job Training** *by Leigh Montville* /74
September 23, 1996 **No Pain, No Gain** *by Jaime Diaz* /78
September 30, 1996 **Crowd Pleaser** *by Jaime Diaz* /82
October 14, 1996 **Jackpot!** *by Gary Van Sickle* /86
October 28, 1996 **Top Cat** *by Rick Reilly* /90

Photo Credits /96

INTRODUCTION

BY JOHN GARRITY

YOU CAN BARELY hear the phone from the flower garden, but you aren't surprised when your wife comes to the patio door and calls your name. "It's the office," she shouts. You wipe your sweaty forehead on your sleeve and shake the topsoil off your fingers. Already your mind is halfway across the country where the young golfer is doing something—*must* be doing something, or they wouldn't be calling.

Or you're on the sideline of a practice field somewhere in the south, watching men in shorts and navel-length tee-shirts rehearse their turns and feints. A public relations intern hands you a cellular phone. "I know you're working on another story," the voice says, "but the kid just made the turn at 9-under...."

It's the fall of 1996, and for a golf writer the usual autumn hues and bracing northerlies are relevant only if they affect the play of a 20-year-old Stanford University dropout named Tiger Woods. A professional golfer for—how long now? Five

SI was on the Tiger beat long before the mania that accompanied his pro debut in Milwaukee.

weeks? Six?—Woods is making fools of the PGA Tour players who smiled knowingly at his brilliant amateur record and said, "Well, there's amateur golf, and then there's *professional* golf."

It turns out that there is yet another, unworldly kind of golf—the kind Woods plays. Drives that turn the usual hazards into fly-over country. Fairway shots that bang off the flagstick. Eagle putts that break twice and still find the hole. If the great Bobby Jones said of Jack Nicklaus, "He plays a game with which I am not familiar," it can be said of Woods that his game has become familiar in record time.

Sports Illustrated has played a major role in that familiarization. Tiger Woods first

Faces in the Crowd

SEPTEMBER 24, 1990

Tiger Woods

CYPRESS, CALIF. Tiger, 14, shot a two-under-par 286 for 72 holes to win a national youth golf tournament at Ridglea Country Club in Fort Worth. He has also won five Junior World titles, including the Optimist International in San Diego last July.

appeared in our pages on September 24, 1990, as a Face in the Crowd—third down, between a powerlifting chemist from Secaucus, New Jersey and an Ohio woman who had won her third straight national karate title. Our first profile of Woods, written by staff writer Tim Crothers, appeared in March 1991, when Woods was 15 and a freshman at Western High School in Anaheim, California. "Standing in the parched fairway on the par-5 18th hole at Los Serranos Country Club," Crothers began his article, "Tiger Woods needed a birdie. So, of course, he wanted an eagle. That's Tiger."

In the same piece, Crothers noted that five years had passed since a black golfer

Six months after Tiger's Face in the Crowd, *SI* shot him with his father Earl for a full-length feature.

had won a Tour event: "Tiger is … aware that he could become the role model for a generation of golfers before he's eligible for his driver's license. But he resists being typecast as a racial pioneer. 'I don't want to be the best black golfer on the Tour,' Tiger says. 'I want to be the best *golfer* on the Tour.' "

"Brash words," wrote Crothers, "from a kid who shaves with tweezers."

Actually, the kid seemed shy and prone to understatement compared to those who had watched him develop. Rudy Duran, the club pro who taught Tiger from age four to 10, said, "I saw a kid who popped out of the womb a Magic Johnson or a Wolfgang Amadeus Mozart. He had talent oozing out of his fingertips." Another of Tiger's childhood golf teachers, John Anselmo, said, "I kid his dad that Tiger is not his, but that he comes from another world. I just hope that I live long enough to see what happens. It's going to be amazing."

Five years have passed, and now the kid is signing multi-million-dollar endorsement contracts the way he used to sign autographs for classmates. The transcendent hype comes not from teaching pros and proud parents, but from nervous touring pros and awed announcers. "He was fifty, sixty yards longer than me," two-time British Open champion Greg Norman said at the 1996 Masters. "I felt very inferior."

Amid what can only be described as Tiger hysteria, we at *Sports Illustrated* have tried to keep our heads. The dozen or so writers whose Woodswork is compiled in this volume have tried not to gush; our photographers have shot their thousands of frames with commendable objectivity. Even the editors have shown restraint, declining to cover Tiger marginalia: the pro basketball games he attends, the girls he dated in college, his routine dental appointments.

Nevertheless, in the fall of '96 Tiger seems to have driven the rest of tournament golf off our pages. The last golfer to do that was Nicklaus, whose name on a leader board on a Saturday invariably caused the names of an *SI* writer and photographer to appear on some airline

Greg Norman is only one of the many experts who have been awed by Tiger's talents.

manifest by nightfall. In the media age, this may be the best measure of an athlete: how many lives one disrupts simply by doing one's thing.

Fortunately, the staff at *Sports Illustrated* thrives on such interruptions.

Which is why, when the phone rings and the voice says, "Tiger is tearing it up in Las Vegas—can you go?"—the answer is almost always, "I'm on my way."

We've got this Tiger by the tale, and we aren't letting go.

ACT I
THE KID

ACT I
THE KID

BY JOHN GARRITY

IT'S NOT OFTEN that writers have picture ideas, but when a *Sports Illustrated* writer says he has an image in mind, the photographer usually listens. That's what contributing photographer Robert Beck was doing one February afternoon at Riviera Country Club in Pacific Palisades, California, site of the Los Angeles Open—listening to the writer, who had an image lodged in his overheated cranium.

"I think I'm going to lead with the kid hitting off the first tee," the writer said, talking to Beck over the gallery ropes on the 11th fairway. "It must be, what, a hundred feet down to the landing area? A shot from above and behind, looking out over this valley of green fairway and eucalyptus trees…" The writer raised a finger for emphasis. "A metaphor! A take-off point for the kid's career."

Beck, a tall man with a sandy mustache and a bright smile, said, "I'll take a look at it."

An hour later, Beck was back—with misgivings. "There's no room to set up behind the tee. But if they'll let me get on top of the clubhouse and shoot down…"

A collaboration between a writer, a photographer and the Man upstairs yielded this memorable shot.

The following afternoon, after negotiating with club authorities, Beck and his assistant took their positions on the edge of the clubhouse roof, overlooking the first tee and the crush of spectators. The perspective was ideal; the light, unfortunately, was not. The sky had been overcast all day, draining Riviera of the rich colors prized by the magazine's photo editors. And Beck knew he might get only one opportunity, because the kid needed a low second-round score to survive the 36-hole cut.

"It was amazing," Beck told the writer later. "Tiger was standing on the tee, shaking hands with everybody, taking his practice swings, and there was no light. But when he was introduced and stepped up to hit, a hole opened up in the clouds and the sun came through."

"So you got it," the writer said.

"Yeah, I got it. The thing is, by the time his ball hit the fairway, the light was bad again. It was like a ten-second window of opportunity, and it opened up for Tiger."

Years later, Tiger's father, Earl Woods, would hear this story and smile knowingly. The boy's career was littered with such phenomena—omens, prescient thoughts, fulfilled prophecies. "It's all being controlled by the Man upstairs," Earl said. "I know that with absolute certainty. Too many things have happened."

To those who covered Tiger Woods from the beginning, there seemed, indeed, to be somebody or something pulling his strings. Most of us assumed it was Earl Woods. He was the prototypical Stage Father, whipping out his wallet with that cute snapshot of a 10-month-old Tiger swinging a vacuum-cleaner attachment. And then you had those stories about the kid shooting a 9-hole 48 at age 2, hitting balls on a national TV show at age 4 and beating touring pros while in junior high—all of which, while verifiable, proved nothing. Child actors rarely achieved stardom as adults.

Funny thing, though: rereading these stories from Tiger's early amateur career, one has to search for the discouraging word—a cautious paragraph here, a note of skepticism there—inserted to protect the author if the kid turned out to be all hat and no cattle.

Seeing Tiger play made believers of most of us.

Even at the age of 15 Tiger was making believers out of the writers who saw him play.

"YOU THE KID!"

By March 1992, the legend of Tiger Woods had begun to take root in the national conscious-ness. Woods had won six junior titles—including a U.S. Junior Amateur—and at 16 was beginning to provoke comparisons to another one-time prodigy named Nicklaus. When the officials at the Los Angeles Open offered Tiger a chance to play in his first PGA tournament, *Sports Illustrated* **dispatched John Garrity to get the story.** *BY JOHN GARRITY*

THE FIRST TEE at Riviera Country Club, on a cliff 75 feet above the fairway, looks more like a jumping-off point for hang gliders than a starting point for golfers. And yet it's a great place from which to launch a drive ... or a career.

High school sophomore Tiger Woods did both last Thursday when he teed off in the first round of the Nissan Los Angeles Open. At 16 years and two months, he became the youngest golfer ever to play in a PGA Tour event—a man-cub among men in a sport that favors the long-in-the-tooth over the teething.

Tiger, the 6' 1" reigning U.S. Junior Amateur champion, stepped to the tee weighing only 140 pounds, and this was following a meal earlier that week of seven pizza slices and a vanilla ice-cream cone. On a typical Thursday morning he would have been sitting in the third row of Glenn Taylor's advanced geometry class at Western High in Anaheim, laboring over angular and perpendicular bisectors. "It's sort of like what he's doing on the golf course," Taylor said after that day's round, "except that out there Tiger's doing it all in his head without a compass."

Beginnings are instructive. Wednesday, in the pro-am, a nervous Tiger had deployed a driver at the majestic 1st tee and hit a high, sweeping hook into the corporate tents, out of bounds. The following morning, in front of a gallery that included hundreds of enthusiastic support-ers, he went with his three-wood and spanked a crowd-pleasing 280-yard draw out over the

Tiger's fluid but explosive swing has elicited oohs and aahs from the very beginning of his career.

17

cliff, the ball stopping in the first cut of left rough on the 501-yard par-5. "I was so tense I had a tough time holding the club," Tiger said later. "It was like rigor mortis had set in."

From there Tiger drilled another three-wood to the middle of the green and got down in two putts for a birdie. On leader boards around the course, the score went up: T. WOODS, -1.

"That was neat," he said afterward.

Following that cue, let's put the events of Tiger's week into two categories:

•NEAT—Playing in the pro-am with pro Gary Hallberg and actor Peter Falk ... getting an encouraging pat from golf legend Sam Snead ... hearing fans shout "You the kid!" ... shooting a first-round, one-over-par 72 to get within reach of the 36-hole cut ... and walking onto the final green late Friday afternoon to a rousing ovation. ("More than a thrill," Tiger said.)

•NOT SO NEAT—The distractions of gallery movement and noise ("I've never had a gallery," Tiger said. "I wasn't used to it.") ... television cameras in his face between shots ... and a 75 on Friday to finish the two rounds at five-over-par 147 and miss the cut by six shots.

"It was a learning experience," Tiger said, relaxed and smiling, when it was over, "and I learned I'm not that good."

Huh? O.K., 17 strokes separated Tiger from second-round leader Davis Love III, who was 12 under. But he was just 12 strokes behind eventual winner Fred Couples, the 1991 PGA Player of the Year. And although Tiger was off his game—he hit only 10 of 36 fairways though he is normally consistent off the tee—he outscored 15 seasoned players, including two-time U.S. Open champion Andy North.... Not exactly a confidence crusher, now is it? More important, Tiger showed that he knows how to scrape it around when he doesn't have his "A" game, which is the mark of a golfer as opposed to a ball striker....

Before he turns pro, [Tiger] says, he wants to win a U.S. Amateur title, play in the Walker Cup, conquer his hummingbird metabolism in order to add weight, lead some lucky college team to the NCAA championship and get an accounting degree. And, oh, yeah, he had a high school match Monday against Gahr High in Anaheim.

"I've got a lot of growing to do, both physically and mentally," Tiger said before leaving Riviera, "but I'll play these guys again—eventually."

He understood: In golf, it's not how fast you get good—it's how good you get.

The impish grin was one of the only indicators of just how young the kid really was.

NO HOLDING THIS TIGER

When Tiger Woods arrived in Portland for the 1993 U.S. Junior Amateur championship, he was the clear favorite, having won the title in both '91 and '92. But Tiger put himself in a treacherous spot in the final, down 2 with two holes to play. Of course, as Tim Crothers reported, the inconceivable had become almost routine for Tiger. *BY TIM CROTHERS*

IS ELDRICK (TIGER) Woods really old enough to have won anything three times already? No way.

Way. Woods, 17, the cocksure golf prodigy from Cypress, California, who tells anybody who asks that all he really wants to be is the Michael Jordan of his sport, mirrored his idol last week by completing a three-peat at the U.S. Junior Amateur in Portland, Oregon. To look at him, Woods seems barely old enough to have three-peated with his razor.

Woods proved once again that he is the best golfer around among those not yet allowed to vote. But while Woods is accustomed to dominating junior events, he narrowly escaped this time. All Woods did was defeat Ryan Armour, 16, in 19 holes by surviving a dormie situation with two holes remaining in the final. Woods birdied the 17th and 18th holes at the Waverley Country Club to pull even and then parred the first extra hole to become the first player to win the championship three times.... "It was the most amazing comeback of my career," said Woods. "I had to play the best two holes of my life under the toughest circumstances, and I did it."

This latest first is nothing new for a young man already first in firsts. Last year he came back from two shots down with six holes to play to become the first golfer to win the junior amateur twice. Two years ago he charged back from a three-hole deficit after six holes to become the first to win the event at such a young age, as well as the first black champion....

Down 2 [in the 1993 final] at the par-4 17th, Woods hit a nine-iron approach shot within eight feet of the pin. As he lined up the birdie putt that, had he missed, would have finished him, Woods called upon another mentor. He muttered to his caddie, Jay Brunza, "Got to be like Nicklaus. Got to will this in the hole." He sank the putt to pull within one.

On the 578-yard par-5 18th, Woods cracked his drive more than 300 yards. "After he airmailed it, he turned around and saw Armour pull out an iron, and Tiger's face hardened," said Woods's father, Earl. "Tiger realized Armour was just trying to make par, and he said to himself, You think I can't birdie this hole? I'll show you what I got."

It wouldn't be easy. Woods's three-iron from the light rough faded into a bunker 40 yards from the green. "I'm thinking, He'll be lucky to get it on the green," said Armour later, "and he knocks it [to within] 10 feet. How good is that?"

Still, with Armour looking at a tap-in par, Woods had to sink yet another birdie putt. He rolled, no, willed the 10-footer in to force the playoff. Woods loudly exhorted himself as he stalked off the green, but the raucous gallery drowned him out.

Sudden death began on number 1, a 333-yard par-4 that Woods had bogeyed in both rounds on Saturday. He hit an iron off the tee and an approach to within 20 feet of the cup. Armour also hit his second shot onto the green—but 60 feet away. Armour would three-putt, missing a tricky downhill

Woods drained a clutch 10-footer on the final hole to force a playoff with Armour.

seven-foot comebacker.

Woods lagged his first putt to within four feet and then sank his second one to win.

Woods's ensuing celebration was the first time he broke his concentration all day. The kid wept as his dad ran onto the green and embraced him. Both men's eyes glazed. Said Earl, "All Tiger could say was, 'I did it, I did it,' and I kept saying, 'I'm so proud of you' over and over. Time stops in moments like that."

THE COMEBACK KID

As the years of his youth increased, so too did the list of Woods-related firsts. In winning his first U.S. Amateur in 1994, Woods added another, this time becoming the first man ever to come from as far behind as six holes and emerge as the amateur champion. Over the next two years the legend would grow larger still.   *BY TIM ROSAFORTE*

ON THE 17TH tee Tiger Woods never gave a second thought to the water surrounding the hole's infamous island green, the landmark of the Tournament Players Club-Sawgrass Stadium course in Ponte Vedra, Florida. In his hands he first held a nine-iron, then exchanged it in favor of a pitching wedge with lead tape on the back. He had 139 yards to the stick, the wind at his back and the heart of a young lion thumping in his chest. His target? "The pin," he would say later. "I was going directly at the pin."

This was to be the defining moment for Woods in a U.S. Amateur comeback victory that bordered on the impossible: six down after 13 holes of the 36-hole match-play final, five down with 12 holes remaining, three down going to the final nine. His opponent was Okla-homa State junior Trip Kuehne, a 22-year-old whose sister Kelli won the U.S. Junior Girls' Championship in July. Kuehne shot a brilliant 66 in the morning round to open the gaping lead, but the 18-year-old Woods would not succumb. At the 16th Woods's birdie evened the match for the first time in 33 holes.

At the par-3 17th, Woods's fearless tee shot landed in a nearly impossible place—to the right of the flagstick, positioned far to the green's right side. The ball first hit just four paces from the water's edge. Woods's mother, Kultida, watching on TV at home in Cypress, California, rolled off her bed and onto the floor as the ball landed. "That boy almost gave me a heart attack," she said. "All I kept saying was, 'God, don't let that ball go in the water.' That boy tried to kill me."

By the time Woods rolled in his dramatic birdie putt on 17 he was solidly "in the zone."

Woods's gutty win produced the first musings about when the kid might decide to turn pro.

The ball spun into the fringe, took a soft bounce into the rough and spun back onto the collar just past pin high and no more than three feet from the water. It seemed as if everybody watching were holding his breath—everybody except Woods, who had faith that a wedge was the right club and that his ball would somehow stay on the green. "You don't see too many pros hit it right of that pin," Kuehne said afterward. "It was a great gamble that paid off."

The ensuing putt, which dropped for a birdie, was in the 14-foot range, but afterward Woods couldn't remember the distance, the break or the grain. He couldn't even remember hitting the putt or the fist-pumping celebration that followed. "I was in the zone," he said.

He stayed in the zone on the par-4 18th, knocking a seven-iron 15 paces from the hole. When Kuehne sent his first putt four feet past the hole and lipped out coming back, it was over; the two friends shook hands, then hugged. Tiger's father, Earl, ... dropped his walking stick and went onto the green. Father and son embraced for what seemed like minutes as applause rained down from the spectators standing on the stadium mounds.

"It's an amazing feeling to come from that many down to beat a great player," said Woods, who became the first player in the tournament's history to come back from as many as six holes down to win. "It's indescribable."

There was more history made on this day, as Woods became the youngest winner of the oldest golf championship in the U.S. His name will go on the Havemayer Trophy alongside those of former Amateur champions like Jack Nicklaus, who is one of five golfers who have won the prestigious U.S. Amateur at the age of 19.

Moreover, Woods became the first black to win this tournament. "When Tiger won his first U.S. Junior [in 1991]," said Earl, "I said to him, 'Son, you have done something no black person in the United States has ever done, and you will forever be a part of history.' But this is ungodly in its ramifications."

For those who follow junior and amateur golf, what Woods did on the Stadium course comes as no surprise. The only three-time winner of the U.S. Junior title, he has been a golfing phenom since he was old enough to pick up a club. In this, his fourth try at the U.S. Amateur, Woods had more than a few close calls. In the round of 16 on Thursday, he was three down with five holes to play against 1986 U.S. Amateur champion Buddy Alexander, now the golf coach at Florida. At the island 17th, Woods needed, and got, a favorable bounce from his tee shot, which ulti-

mately nestled in the rough two feet from the water. Woods had watched that ball in the air, hooking instead of fading, and, as he said later, "I nearly passed out." Boosted by Alexander's collapse—he failed to make par on any of the last six holes—Woods came back to win....

Woods still has to register for the fall semester as a freshman at Stanford.... [But] it will not become any easier for Tiger, or his parents, to ignore the lure of the pro tour, especially now that he has been stamped with the undeniable look of a future superstar. Curiously, it was a victory that almost never happened. Woods's 11th-hour heroics in the Amateur actually began three weeks ago. After Woods won the Western Amateur in Benton Harbor, Michigan, he and his father dashed to Chicago for a flight to California, where Tiger had to qualify for the U.S. Amateur the next morning in Chino Hills. However, traffic on the way to O'Hare turned a 90-minute drive into a three-hour ordeal, and the Woodses missed their plane. They had to stand by for the last flight out, knowing that if Tiger didn't get on that plane, he would not make his tee time—and would not be able to compete in the Amateur.

"I prayed, and my prayers were answered," says Earl. "Thank God we got on that damn airplane."

OCTOBER 17, 1994

TALE OF A TIGER

Just one month after his U.S. Amateur triumph Tiger Woods was a winner again, this time at the World Amateur Team Championship, where he charmed the French audiences who flocked to see the new American sensation. In the first round, Woods had four bogeys but then, as usual, made a dramatic turnaround with an eagle-birdie finish to salvage a 70. Later, Woods quoted Chip Beck's comment before the final day of the 1993 Ryder Cup: "The will to win can overcome mechanical breakdowns." *BY JAIME DIAZ*

HAVING PANNED THE largest amateur golf gold nuggets in his own country this year, 18-year-old U.S. Amateur champion Tiger Woods journeyed to the outskirts of Paris last week in search of treasure in the shadow of the gilded Palace of Versailles. The result: He unearthed another hefty lode of confidence and experience in helping the U.S. win its first World Amateur Team Championship in a dozen years.

The Americans' 11-stroke victory over runner-up Great Britain & Ireland was indisputably led by flinty Allen Doyle, whose 72-hole total of 277 was the low individual score in the biennial competition, which this year attracted four-man teams from 45 countries. On Sunday, the 46-year-old Doyle made up for a bogey, triple bogey start with a heroic six-under-par run over the final seven holes.

"I felt awful," he said of his 40 on the front nine, "but I was damned if I wasn't going to come scratching back." And so, with the U.S. trailing by four strokes with nine holes to play, he fired a 30 on the back nine to spark the runaway victory.

But Woods also had his claws out, shooting a 72 on Sunday despite the pressure of playing in the tournament's final threesome. "I thought batting cleanup would suit Tiger to a tee," said Doyle. "He already had the crowd, and the young man is not afraid of pressure."

"I loved it," said Woods, whose rounds of 70-75-67-72 (sixth individually) all counted toward the team score in a format that tallied a team's best three rounds each day. "My only thought was to hit solid golf shots all day long. Nothing can go wrong then."

Tiger La Terreur gained further valuable experience on the fairways of France.

Almost nothing has gone wrong for Woods in his meteoric golf career. As a superstar amateur—he is the only player to win three straight U.S. Junior Amateur championships, the only player to win both the U.S. Junior and the Amateur and the youngest player ever to win the Amateur—he is galvanizing interest in amateur golf for the first time in decades.

In Versailles, Woods was clearly the star, drawing galleries larger than those of all the French golfers combined. The Gallic press celebrated him as much as it has any American since Jerry Lewis. The sports daily *L'Equipe* called him TIGER LA TERREUR, while the daily *Le Figaro* compared him with another prodigy—Mozart....

For all the fluidity and power of Woods's game, it is his mental toughness that appears to be his greatest weapon. As each success brings higher expectations—not to mention the temptation to leave college, turn professional and mine real gold—it is Woods's inner strength that will have to hold him in good stead. "As talented as he is, Tiger's going to have to be better with his head than with his hands," says Doyle. "What I really like about him is that he knows that he's a long way from where he wants to get to. In golf, the way you get better is by knowing you're not there."

In the case of Tiger Woods, he might get closer to "there" than anyone yet.

ACT II
THE AMATEUR

ACT II

THE AMATEUR

BY JOHN GARRITY

IF TIGER WOODS has a Boswell, it is *Sports Illustrated* senior writer Jaime Diaz. "Famously disorganized" would be a good description for Diaz, who is known at the magazine for his late and muddled expense reports, his ability to sleep on hard surfaces and his tendency to stagger to deadlines like the last finisher in a marathon. The paradox of Diaz is that he is one of *SI*'s most orderly thinkers. His prose suggests hours of calm reflection, as if its creator worked with a pipe in one hand, a fire crackling nearby.

Diaz has no trouble remembering his first meeting with Tiger Woods. "I met him in the parking lot of the Coto de Caza Golf Club, near Irvine, when he was 14," he recalls. "I had been reading about this California phenom, so I called up Earl and made a date to play golf with them. In the parking lot, Tiger was very reticent. Not sullen, just quiet. I mostly talked to Earl."

On the first hole, Diaz outdrove Tiger, flexing some of the muscles he once displayed as a member of the University of San Francisco golf team. Gradually, the youngster warmed up to the journalist, and by the 18th hole Tiger was ready for some serious action. He

By the time Tiger reached Stanford, he was already the reigning U.S. Amateur champion.

said, "I'll play you for some ABC gum."

"I didn't know what that was," says Diaz, "but I knew it couldn't be much. He was 14."

The writer took the bet, the kid birdied the hole, and the piper had to be paid.

"Okay," said Diaz. "What's ABC gum?"

With a sly smile, Tiger replied, "Already Been Chewed."

The irony of Tiger's prank is not lost on anyone who has written a Woods story since August, 1994. Finding undigested bits of Tiger lore has become a cottage industry for newspapermen and TV researchers. At *SI*, senior writer Rick Reilly set a high standard with his March 1995 piece, "Goodness Gracious, He's a Great Ball of Fire," and it has been Jaime's sometimes thankless task to erect new insights on an already mountainous body of Woods analysis. To that end—and because he genuinely liked the kid—Jaime played catch with Tiger, pored over scrapbooks with his parents, and tried not to get between the ravenous Tiger and the buffet line when they ate at the local Sizzler.

"I rarely interviewed him," Diaz says. "I did the journalism more or less on the sly, just talking with him. He finally decided I wasn't going to misquote him or trap him, and we got to be pretty close."

When Tiger played in his first Masters, dogged every step by reporters, it was Diaz who got to debrief him daily in the Crow's Nest, the clubhouse dormitory for amateurs. When journalists were speculating that Tiger *might* turn pro the week after the 1996 U.S. Amateur, Diaz was in his cluttered hotel room, tapping out confirmed details like "Nike," "Titleist," and "37 million dollars."

For all the effort he's put in, Diaz's take on Woods hasn't changed much since that first round of golf, six years ago. "I was impressed with how smart he was. How aware. How articulate." His visit to the Woods house, later that same day, left him just as impressed with Kultida, Tiger's mother. "Earl is sort of a playmate and mentor to Tiger, but his mom is really the hard rock, his conscience and discipline. And when it comes to household chores, homework, schedules, practice sessions—you name it—Tiger is very disciplined."

Unlike some writers we know.

As Tiger considered his professional options, Diaz was there to record his every thought.

GOODNESS GRACIOUS, HE'S A GREAT BALL OF FIRE

By March 1995 we had heard all about the amazing comebacks, the Daly-like distance and the awe-inspiring shotmaking that were integral to the game of Tiger Woods. But now, with Rick Reilly's memorable piece, we had the definitive story on how this astonishing talent came to be. Soon the legend would be put to the test against golf's best. *BY RICK REILLY*

WHEN THE BOY was six, he asked his parents for the subliminal tape. In the parents' plan to raise the greatest golfer who ever lived, the boy's mind had to be trained. The tape was all rippling brooks and airy flutes on top and chest-thumpers underneath:

MY DECISIONS ARE STRONG!
I DO IT ALL WITH MY HEART!
From the beginning, the boy understood what the tape was for, and he liked it. A regular Freud of the first grade. He would pop in the tape while swinging in front of the mirror or putting on the carpet or watching videos of old Masters tournaments. In fact, he played the tape so often that it would have driven any other parents quite nuts. Any *other* parents.

He took the messages that came with the tape and tacked them to the wooden bookshelf in his tiny room. All the people from *That's Incredible* and *Eye on L.A.* and *The Mike Douglas Show* who tracked in and out to meet the Great Black Hope, they all missed the messages. But there they were, right under their very ears.

I FOCUS AND GIVE IT MY ALL!
When the boy was seven, his parents installed the psychological armor. If he had a full wedge shot, the father would stand 15 feet in front of him and say, "I'm a tree." And the kid would have to hit over him. The father would

Woods's trip to Europe for the 1994 World Amateur Championship included a stop at Versailles.

jingle his change before the boy's bunker shots. Pump the brake on the cart on the boy's mid-irons. Rip the Velcro on his glove over a three-footer.

What his dad tried to do, whenever possible, was cheat, distract, harass and annoy him. You spend 20 years in the military, train with the Green Berets, do two tours of Nam and one of Thailand, you learn a few things about psychological warfare.

It was not good enough that by age two the boy could look at a grown man's swing and understand it ("Look, Daddy," he would say, "that man has a reverse pivot!"); that by three he was beating 10-year-olds; that by five he was signing autographs (because he couldn't write script, he printed his name in block letters); that by six he'd already had two holes in one. No, the father knew his son would need a mind as one-piece as his swing....

He was the father's one-boy battalion. Before tournaments the father would tell him to make sure his gear was in "tip-top shape, lie and loft." The father made sure the boy "understood the mission" (win). He would hold "debriefings" after the tournament (talk about how it went). What the father wanted for his son was the one thing he had had in battle, the thing that had kept Charlie from putting him in a bag: a "dark side," as he calls it, "a coldness." It was coldness that had allowed him to storm a VC-held village and step over dead men without swallowing hard. It had helped him to charge on against tracer fire without blinking when his every nerve screamed, "Get down!"

And so the boy learned coldness too. Eventually, nothing the father did could make him flinch. The boy who once heard subliminal messages under rippling brooks now couldn't hear a thing. Once at a tournament a marshal's walkie-talkie went off at volume 10 out of 10 during the boy's backswing. The boy admitted later that he never heard it.

"I wanted to make sure," says the father, "he'd never run into anybody who was tougher mentally than he was."...

MY WILL MOVES MOUNTAINS!

By second grade the boy had a nationally known name—Tiger Woods—and he had already played in, and won, his first international tournament, against kids from all over the world. His father took him to the 1st tee, where all the other nervous little boys and hyperventilating dads had gone. And he said, "Son, I want you to know I love you no matter how you do. Enjoy yourself." And then Tiger stepped up and hit a

By the time Tiger was 15, Earl had him approaching each shot with single-minded concentration.

perfect drive. And after the round was over, the father asked him what he was thinking about as he stood over that first shot.

And Tiger said, simply, "Where I wanted my ball to go, Daddy." Not: *Don't miss it, don't skull it, don't fail.* Only: *Where I wanted my ball to go.*

"That's when I knew," says Earl Woods, the father. "That's when I knew how good he was going to be."

I BELIEVE IN ME!

From the beginning the idea was synergy: Produce a thing greater than the sum of its parts. But how? He and she were so opposite.

Lucky legacy: Woods's good looks are based on an eclectic mix of ethnic backgrounds.

He was 37. She was 23. He was a quarter American Indian, a quarter Chinese and half black. She was half Thai, a quarter Chinese and a quarter white. He was from Manhattan, Kansas. She was from Bangkok. He was a paid killer. She was a peaceful civilian. He was a Protestant. She was a Buddhist. He had raised himself. She came from a wealthy family. Both of his parents had died by the time he was 13. She still lived with hers.

Raise a wonder child? They could barely hook up for a first date. He was on assignment in Thailand, and she was working as a secretary in a U.S. Army office. He said eight, thinking p.m. She heard eight, thinking a.m. "Thai girls *not* go out at night," she says proudly. When she didn't show up, he figured she had stiffed him. When he didn't show up, she went and found him....

They moved to Brooklyn, where they were married in 1969, and then to Cypress, California, where in 1975 she bore him a son, the First Son, in Asia the most important child, the one responsible for the family as soon as he's able. It was also her last child, since she suffered complications during the delivery. Together, the two of them, Earl and Tida, the two opposites, his yang to her yin, put all their love in one babbling, smiling, golf-swinging basket.

Maybe it's true: The hybrid rose is stronger than the two strains. They tended it as if it were the last rose in the garden. In his 18 years under their roof, Tiger never once had a baby-sitter. "I let my husband go," Tida says. "I stay with Tiger. Tiger more important than a party."... In their love for him they were equally devout, but they stuck to their roles. Earl was the best friend. Tida was the parent. Earl was the road buddy. Tida was waiting at home. Earl wouldn't spank the boy. Tida would. Earl let him make his mistakes. Tida punished him....

I WILL MY OWN DESTINY!
Even the name was part of the plan. Eldrick (Tiger) Woods. The "Eldrick" was made up out of the blue by Tida, because it joined the first letters of her husband's first name, Earl, and hers, Kutida. You understand? No matter what, we will always be at your side.

The "Tiger" was given to him by his father in honor of his father's Vietnam combat partner, Nguyen Phong of the South Vietnamese army. Earl nicknamed Phong "Tiger" for his unblinking bravery. It was Tiger who took him on an insane mission through the streets of a VC-held village and got himself the Vietnamese silver star for it. It was Tiger, his best friend, who pulled him off a rice-paddy dike seconds after sniper fire tore over him. Around 1967 or '68 they lost contact but Earl is convinced Tiger is still alive somewhere in the world. And so he nicknamed his own son Tiger in hopes that someday Nguyen Phong would pick up a newspaper and read about Earl's famous son, the greatest golfer who ever lived, and understand....

The Woodses break every stage-parent rule ever written. When dads drag their seven-year-olds up to Wayne Gretzky and say, "Wayne, will you tell him he's got to practice," Gretzky always says, "Nobody ever told me to practice." The same is true for Tiger Woods. Not once did Earl or Tida insist that he get in his golf practice. The trick was getting him home....

MY STRENGTH IS GREAT
At 16, when the boy had surpassed his father's knowledge, the father brought in the PGA Tour swing coach from Houston. Talk about pressure. [Butch] Harmon, caretaker of Greg Norman's game, suddenly had Thomas Edison walk into his electronics school....

Now Harmon can't get rid of the kid. "He wants to work with me 24 hours a day," the teacher says. "I can't get him off the phone."

I SMILE AT OBSTACLES!
When the Great Black Hope goes to the Augusta National Golf Club in two weeks as the most-anticipated young black player ever to walk through its clubhouse doors, there will be only one weird thing.

He isn't black.

Well, he is a quarter black. But mostly he is Thai, and partly he is Chinese, and Tida wants you to know it. "All the media try to put black in him," she says, rising off the couch. "Why don't they ask who half of Tiger is from? In United States, one little part black is *all black*. Nobody want to listen to me. I been trying to explain to people, but they don't understand. To say he is 100 percent black is to deny his heritage. To deny his grandmother and grandfather. To deny *me*!"...

"I don't want to be the best black golfer ever," he has said a hundred times. "I want to be the best *golfer* ever."...

I AM FIRM IN MY RESOLVE!
At 18, he traded millions for a dorm room and no sleep.

Most any night you catch Tiger Woods and his roommate at Stanford, you'll notice Woods is not calling his agent, not getting a massage and not checking his investments. Usually, he is doing what his roomie is doing—cramming for a test and trying like hell to keep his hands off the TV remote....

"Money can't buy us," Tida says proudly. What she and Earl want for Tiger is an education.... "What he need money for?" she says. "If you turn him pro, you take his youth away from him."...

Earl and Tida may need an extra wing on their home to accommodate all of Tiger's trophies.

I FULFILL MY RESOLUTIONS POWERFULLY!
Today some of the worst rainstorms of the past decade are pelting the Bay Area. There are floods and mud slides and even a few deaths. Earl and Tida are a little worried, especially because when they give the First Son a call, just to see if he's O.K., there's no answer.

No wonder. Tiger isn't somewhere safe. He is out here, alone, on the 10th hole of the closed Stanford golf course, in the middle of a horizontal wave of rain, his car the only one in the lot, and he is ripping two-irons into the teeth of an Auntie Em wind, getting ready for what he might face at St. Andrews. No coach ordered him here. No parent. No schedule. Hey, you don't get lucky and get this kind of horrible weather every day. *Expect the best, prepare for the worst.* And as the rain narrows his eyes and the gale wobbles his stance, you can't help noticing that he is smiling, a lifetime of subliminal messages happily at work.

OUT OF SIGHT

When Tiger Woods made his Masters debut in 1995, Jaime Diaz was there to record the historic event. As he had so often, Woods responded to the pressure brilliantly, averaging an eye-popping 311.1 yards per drive, finishing as the low amateur and, at one point in the third round, flirting with the fabled Augusta leader board. *BY JAIME DIAZ*

IT SURELY SAYS something significant about Tiger Woods that in a week in which he 1) was low amateur in his first Masters, 2) made his first cut in seven tries in a PGA Tour-sanctioned event, 3) drew history-hungry throngs that ran the gamut from Lee Elder to Shoal Creek founder Hall Thompson, 4) got rave reviews from every top pro who saw him play, 5) hit some talent shots destined to become part of the tournament's lore and 6) kept his conduct above reproach under a media microscope that covered every move of the first black amateur ever to play in the racially complicated atmosphere of the Masters, the 19-year-old Stanford freshman was still disappointed when it became clear on Saturday that he could not win the tournament.

Half an hour after holing out for a third-round 77 that had put him five over par and 15 strokes behind the leaders, Woods laid his lanky 6'1", 150-pound frame on a worn but comfortable green sofa in the Crow's Nest, a cozy room that is topped by the cupola of Augusta National's clubhouse. "I'm so frustrated," said Woods. Birdies on the 2nd and 3rd holes had gotten him to two under for the tournament and on the verge of going on the leader board. But then a spate of bogeys, punctuated by a 6 on the par-5 8th hole when he took 4 from the edge of the green, turned the round into a struggle.

But rather than mope, Woods's face took on a knowing smile, the kind a smart kid gets when he has run into something that is, for the moment, bigger than he is. On Sunday he came back with a solid 72, birdieing three of

Woods looked eminently relaxed strolling down the fairways with Norman and Price (right).

the last four holes for a total of 293, five over, to finish 41st.

"The way I drove it and putted, I know I could have been in the hunt," said Woods, longingly watching the telecast of the third-round leaders finishing their rounds. "I guess everyone feels that way, but I feel like this place is perfect for me. I guess I need to get to know it better."

He paused and gestured toward the black-and-white framed photographs of Masters champions hanging on the walls. "Someday," he said, the smile growing tighter, "I'm going to get my picture up there."

It would be easy to dismiss such talk as a young man's delusions of grandeur. After all, when confronted with the most essential challenge that the Masters presents, hitting the precise landing areas on Augusta National's rolling greens, Woods was unable to consistently deliver, even with short iron and wedge approaches. Critics could choose to consider the first official putt of Woods's Masters career—a 30-footer on the 1st hole that trundled past the cup, off the green and down an embankment before stopping 50 feet from the hole—as an ugly harbinger. They might also point out that both Ben Crenshaw in 1972 and Phil Mickelson in 1991 did better in their Augusta debuts as amateurs. They could make a case that the reigning U.S. Amateur champion is becoming a victim of hype.

They would be wrong, however, because to dismiss Woods's performance as anything but extraordinary would be to miss the point. For if Woods proved one thing last week, it is that despite whatever sociological baggage anyone cares to impose, he and the Masters are a perfect fit. Although Tiger's excellent adventure was satisfying on many levels, it was most important as a reconnaissance mission to lay the groundwork for many future trips to—and almost surely some victories in—Augusta.

The fact is, based on the manner in which he played if not necessarily his score, Woods brought a unique energy to the 59th Masters. From his first practice round on Monday to his early finish on Sunday, [Woods] showed a talent for the game every bit as electrifying as that of the young Nicklaus and the young Ballesteros, both of whom also came to their first Masters at the age of 19.

With the impassive aplomb with which he bombed his opening tee shot on all four days within wedge distance of the 1st green, Woods demonstrated that he feels frighteningly comfortable at Augusta. For emphasis Woods made another statement after Saturday's third round while on the practice range next to eventual runner-up Davis Love III. When Love, the longest hitter on the Tour last year, pulled out his driver, the spectators in the bleachers cheered and loudly urged him to try to carry the 50-foot-high netting, some 260 yards away, that is designed to keep balls from going onto Washington Road, a main thoroughfare that abuts the range. After Love failed on two attempts, Woods shyly asked, "Should I try?" When Love nodded, Woods unsheathed his Cobra oversized driver to the delight of the spectators. Woods then smoothly rocked into his compact backswing and ripped a perfectly straight cannon shot that easily cleared the netting, causing the stands to erupt and drawing a smile from every player on the range.

If such feats have little to do with shooting low scores, Woods's practice-round partners at

Woods was unfailingly polite with the hordes of young fans who followed him everywhere.

Stunningly long off the tees and fairways, Woods was never out of reach of the Augusta greens.

the Masters—a formidable collection including Nick Faldo, Raymond Floyd, Greg Norman, Fred Couples, Nick Price and Gary Player—each said that the young man possesses as near to a complete package as they have ever seen in a player his age. All of the veterans are acutely aware of the precariousness of early success in their sport, yet all said that Woods possesses something extra, both physically and in his mental approach to the game….

"The first time I saw Jack Nicklaus or Arnold Palmer or Ben Hogan or Sam Snead or Lee Trevino, I saw something special," [said Player]. "As soon as I saw Tiger Woods swing today, I thought, Man, this young guy has got it. 'It' is something indescribable. It's the way he puts his hands on the club, the way he stands over the ball. It's agility, it's speed. 'It' is what a great horse has."…

Asked on Wednesday what kind of finish he thought would constitute a good tournament

for Tiger, Norman said, "Probably to win, for him. He is good enough...."

So calm was Woods that he had no problem acknowledging and, after his rounds, interacting with a public that clearly found him appealing. Woods's presence attracted more black spectators than ever to the Masters, and he made an effort to fulfill what he seemed to sense was a special responsibility.... At 6 p.m. Friday, after making the cut at even-par 144, Woods and his father drove to a nearby public course, Forest Hills, where Tiger put on a free clinic for caddies and junior golfers. It was his way of honoring Augusta National's black caddies, who, until 1982, were used exclusively in the Masters....

As Woods, surrounded by aging men and young children, hit crisp five-irons off turf nearly devoid of grass, his father announced over a microphone to the crowd, "This young man this week has passed from adolescence to manhood. I'm very proud of him."

"Thanks, Pop," said his son, who will surely be the man to contend with the next time he returns to the Masters.

OUT OF THE WOODS

The two months that followed Woods's first Masters appearance in April brought a new group of Tiger-doubters out of the woodwork, this time the nay-sayers who claimed that Tiger's young, relatively frail frame would be unable to endure the rigors of intense competition. As Jaime Diaz reported, Woods gave his answer to the critics where he always shone brightest—on the golf course. *BY JAIME DIAZ*

THE LAST TIME we saw Tiger Woods, he was withdrawing from the second round of the U.S. Open with a sprained left wrist, visibly weary from the effects of a long college season and the academic demands at Stanford. But the Woods who showed up at the Western Open last week was a giddy 19-year-old embarking on an excellent summer vacation—healthy, clear of mind and eager to play with the big boys again.

Woods performed ably, shooting 74-71 to make his first 36-hole cut ever in a regular PGA Tour event (the Western was his eighth such event over the last three years). He followed with a 77 on Saturday, then rebounded on Sunday with his best Tour round ever, a 69, to finish in 57th place, 12 strokes out of the lead. Woods then rushed off for his first-ever trip to Scotland—where he believes he just might do some damage in the Scottish and British Opens.

While in Chicago, Woods worked to quiet speculation on two fronts, the first being general concern that his gangly, 6' 1", 150-pound frame was in danger of breaking down under the force of his swing and the weight of his heavy playing schedule. Before his injury at Shinnecock—incurred on a hard swing from the rough—Woods in the last two years had undergone a knee operation and suffered from occasional back pain. But last week he insisted he has no chronic physical problems. "The wrist is fine," he said. "I don't have any lingering pain. I'm still growing into my body, and as I get stronger, the less I'll get hurt."

Woods also made it clear that the one-day suspension he received from Stanford for an

Woods looked well rested after making his first 36-hole cut ever in a regular PGA Tour event.

NCAA violation—he kept a diary of his week at the Masters for two golf publications—was perplexing to him but would not affect his plan to remain an amateur until he obtains his degree. "I won't turn pro until 1998, after college," said Woods. "The only thing that's annoying about the NCAA is trying to get used to the rules and regulations, because I've been used to one governing body, the USGA. But it's not going to force me out, no."

Once he got on the fairways and greens of Cog Hill, Woods looked more relaxed than he had in a while. After taking his last final at Stanford, on June 9, Woods returned to his parents' home in Cypress, California, to decompress. He spent most of his time kicking back with childhood friends, his most ambitious project being a 60-mile bike ride along the coast to Laguna Beach....

At Cog Hill, Woods's mission was to work on flattening his swing plane, the latest advice to him from his personal coach, Butch Harmon. The shallower plane should result in a lower, more penetrating trajectory on his iron shots, allowing Woods to have more command in the wind. "The next challenge for me is distance control," says Woods.

Not that Woods has lost any of his phenomenal length with his driver. At Cog Hill, Woods's four-round average of 292.6 yards was the third best in the field.

Woods can hardly wait to unleash his driver on the wide, firm fairways of St. Andrews, but he is even more eager to test his revamped iron game in the gales that blow off the Firth of Forth. "All I can do is keep trying to get better," said Woods after his frustrating third-round 77. "But every day is about making little adjustments, taking what you've got on that day and finding the way to deal with it."

If Woods can make the sort of adjustments at St. Andrews that he made Sunday in the Western, the young star may produce some historic rocking in the cradle of golf.

ENCORE! ENCORE!

The second U.S. Amateur championship won by Tiger Woods was in some ways his least dramatic. But the event was nonetheless significant for the terrifying discovery made by Tim Rosaforte and the other observers at the tournament: that Woods had actually added *new* weapons to his already awe-inspiring arsenal. *BY TIM ROSAFORTE*

"I'M GOING TO make a prediction," Earl Woods said Sunday night, as champagne both tingled and loosened his tongue. "Before he's through, my son will win 14 major championships."

America's most prominent golf father clutched the Havemeyer Trophy, from which he was drinking, and looked around the nearly empty merchandise tent near the clubhouse of the Newport (R.I.) Country Club. The handful of friends and autograph seekers laughed and cheered. His son, 19-year-old Tiger Woods, smiled too—but bashfully. It's embarrassing when Dad blurts out your own secret thoughts.

Skeptics will complain that the Stanford sophomore has yet to win his *first* major championship. But after last week's 95th U.S. Amateur Championship, Earl Woods had every right to see his son's future through

rose-colored champagne glasses. On the same Rhode Island layout where Charles Blair Mac-Donald won the first Amateur in 1895, Tiger Woods became the ninth player to win back-to-back Amateur championships and the first since Bobby Jones to give the impression that he might win as many as he enters. "To my son, Tiger," Earl Woods said, raising the trophy with a stiff right arm. "One of the greatest golfers in the history of the United States."

The father said it boldly. The son had said it already, two hours earlier, with a lightning bolt—an eight-iron to within 18 inches of the cup on the 36th hole of his final match with George (Buddy) Marucci, a luxury-car dealer from Berwyn, Pennsylvania. With Marucci one down but on the green with a 20-foot birdie putt, Woods hit the type of knockdown shot from 140 yards that wasn't in his arsenal at last year's Amateur or earlier this year in

The links-style Newport course challenged Woods to hit an array of precision shots.

his first Masters. At Newport, his knockdown approach to the 18th green flew right over the flag and spun back almost to the cup...

Playing the Scottish Open at Carnoustie and the British Open at St. Andrews in July taught Woods that there was more to hitting golf shots than hitting them full bore. Having a full complement of shots is a prerequisite for playing Newport, a links-style course whose swirling seaside winds shift more often than a running back in a multiple-set offense. And by the time he arrived for the Amateur, Woods had learned how to control his ball in the wind, how to hit a three-quarter draw to a back-left pin, and how to whistle a low two-

iron 265 yards—as he did off the final tee on Sunday. But the knockdown shot was Woods's knockout punch at Newport....

The kid also knows how to pop his father's emotional cork. As they did last year in Florida, when Tiger became the youngest Amateur champion ever, father and son indulged in a long, tearful bear hug on the 18th green. A couple of hours later, as Tiger calmly autographed posters for fans, the old man seemed ready to anoint Jack Nicklaus as "the first Tiger Woods."

You had to forgive Earl. With 14 major championships practically in the bag, a celebration was in order.

51

A Fast Study

A story on Tiger Woods before his second Masters offered Jaime Diaz an opportunity to analyze the growth in Woods's game and to ponder the question that seemed to be on everyone's mind in the golfing world: When would Tiger turn pro? *BY JAIME DIAZ*

TIGER WOODS MIGHT seem to be momentarily parked between a storied past and a golden future, but as he prepares for the 1996 Masters, a glance at his life reveals a young man evolving so quickly, he could qualify as a walking study in time-lapse photography.

During the college-am portion of the recent Southwestern Intercollegiate at the North Ranch Country Club in Westlake Village, California, the 20-year-old Stanford sophomore showed himself to be a work in progress who has grown in three dimensions since his memorable first appearance at the Masters 12 months ago.

First, he is bigger. Since winning the U.S. Amateur last August, Woods has gained 15 pounds, as hormones, training-table cuisine and a weightlifting program have combined to build up his heretofore wispy 6' 2" frame to 155 pounds. His shoulders are wider and his forearms thicker. Woods is also becoming a polished ambassador of the game. Far from the reticent and self-contained stripling who was taken aback by the rush of media that met his debut at Augusta National, Woods now handles himself in public with aplomb. His amateur partners at North Ranch, a boisterous threesome of middle-aged men from the home club who each donated a few hundred dollars to college golf for the privilege of playing with the game's leading prince, loved hitting their popgun drives and immediately blurting things like, "I hope you learned something from that one, Tiger!" Woods played the amiable straight man, all the while responding to the gallery's autograph and photo requests with a pleasant "No problem." It was a performance straight from the book of ... Arnold Palmer.

Bigger, stronger, smarter: The new Tiger was an even more impressive specimen of golfing genius.

Finally, he is a better golfer. Woods is quickly transforming himself from an untamed young gun to a mature shotmaker. While his increased strength allows him to hit his tee shots even farther than he could as the statistically longest hitter over four rounds at the '95 Masters, ... there is now an educated restraint to his driving that makes his mishits much more playable. The gearing down is even more noticeable in his iron play. Whereas Woods used to favor high-flying approaches that were majestic but hard to control, he has developed a shot that flies lower, curves less and carries less spin. He is also hitting his clubs shorter distances with shallower divots, all in the interest of accuracy, consistency and control.

The Tiger Woods who will attack Augusta National this week is much more than a young amateur who will be happy just to play on the weekend.... If Woods does do well at Augusta, it will fuel speculation that he is on the verge of reneging on his vow to postpone his professional career until he gets a degree. In addition to the level of his game and the millions in endorsements he should receive the moment he turns pro, there are plenty of reasons to believe Woods is not long for college golf. For one, unlike last year's Stanford team, which lost the NCAA title to Oklahoma State in a sudden-death playoff, this year's Cardinal is no powerhouse. Woods admits he gets no particular thrill out of week-in, week-out college competition. "I keep myself interested by working on my own game," he says....

Earl and Kultida Woods have softened their original imperative that their son graduate before turning pro. Kultida worries that the academic and athletic demands on Tiger are becoming too stressful. "I will support whatever he decides," she says. "I give him my advice that money is not the issue and to be careful not to sacrifice his youth. But my boy is a man now, and I trust his judgment."...

"Stanford is like utopia," [Woods] says. "It's not the real world, which I guess is why I want to spend more time here. Maybe my game is ready, but the question is, am I ready mentally and emotionally to live the life of a pro?..."

Of course, getting in the hunt on Sunday at the Masters would even further convince Woods that he has simply become too good a golfer to stay in college. Ironically, by preparing hard for the week, Woods is doing everything in his power to end his self-described utopia....

Woods is just eager to see how far he has come in the last 12 months. "That's what I'm looking forward to the most," he says. "Augusta is going to tell me where I am."

The fairways and stately pines of Augusta offered Woods an opportunity to gauge his progress.

IN HIS SIGHTS

It was almost becoming ho-hum. Another week, another triumph for Tiger Woods—this time at the NCAA golf championship in Chattanooga—and as soon as the win was in the bank the speculation about his future began again with renewed fervor. Never mind the semi-collapse in the final round, how long could Woods remain in the amateur ranks, where he had clearly run out of competition? For now, the future would have to wait; Tiger had to hurry back to Stanford to cram for finals. *BY WILLIAM F. REED*

THE FIRST NCAA golf championship was held in 1897, so it was somewhat newsworthy that last week's tournament at the Honors Course, 25 miles east of Chattanooga, set an attendance record. But before you conclude that interest in college golf is rising, you should know that of the 14,694 tickets purchased, roughly 14,000 were bought by people who came to see if Tiger Woods of Stanford really is the best amateur golfer to stroll down a fairway since that fat kid, name of Nicklaus, was at Ohio State from 1958 to '61. The answer, to use the local vernacular, was, "Sure 'nuff."

On each of the four days you didn't have to look long to find Woods.... How big has Tiger become? Well, bigger than the NCAA Championships. Instead of the usual three guards per threesome, his group had nine until the final day, when the number grew to 15. The NCAA, which issued 80 media credentials for last year's championships, in which Woods tied for fifth, passed out 225 for this one. The nightly tournament wrap-up was faxed to 116 recipients, from ESPN's *SportsCenter* to Pro Golf Discount of Birmingham. Almost everywhere Woods turned, somebody asked him to sign a hat or a scorecard. Upon receiving Tiger's autograph after Saturday's final round, one Southern belle said, "Woooo, you have a famous-looking signature. Yeah, I think you're definitely going to be famous." That made Woods grin his million-dollar grin,

No one could blame Woods if he was finding it easier to read his putts than to settle his future.

A streak of uncharacteristically poor shots forced Woods to scramble for his life on Saturday.

which was no small accomplishment considering how angry he was after just shooting an uncharacteristic eight-over-par 80.

For three glorious days the course had been putty in Tiger's hands. He opened on Wednesday with a three-under-par 69 that put him a shot off the lead; took control in Thursday's second round with a 67 that broke the competitive course record held by three players, one of them a Nicklaus (Gary, not Jack); and separated himself from the field with a 69 on Friday that gave him a nine-shot lead heading into the final round. His play was so sweet, so pure, so smart—he often sacrificed distance off the tee to make sure he was on the right side of the fairway—that some people found it amusing when Woods insisted after the third round that the course and the field were not pushovers. "Is it easy out there?" he said, repeating a question with a look of incredulity. "Oh, god, no! This is not a course that you can play aggressively. I feel good about my game, but there's still one more day. Anything can happen."

And doggone if anything—or something or everything—didn't jump up and bite him in Saturday's final round. After reaching the 9th tee at one under for the day, Woods lost seven strokes to par during a five-hole stretch. He came unraveled at number 9, a 369-yard par-4 protected by water along the front of the green. Woods hit a good drive but pushed his second shot into the gallery on the back right side of the hole. He then attempted a flop shot that flew on him and went into the water. Another flop shot left him on the fringe. From there, he two-putted for a triple-bogey 7. Woods then bogeyed 10, 11, 12 and 13. On the PGA Tour that would be fatal 99% of the time. All it did to Woods was cut his margin of victory to four shots (285 to 289) over Rory Sabbatini of Arizona....

For [Woods] the NCAA title was a rite of passage, marking the end of the phenom part of his career and the beginning of the grown-up part. From now on, everything he does in amateur competition will be pretty much redundant. Still, this wasn't the way he wanted to win his first NCAA title. All his final-round fizzle proved, of course, is that he's human. At the news conference on Saturday, he looked drained. "Things started to slip away quickly. I knew that they could," he said. "People will never know what it took for me to get it back. I dug down awfully deep today, and I'm proud of myself."...

Except for a few stray shots on Saturday, he played a brand of golf that renewed interest in some oft-asked questions: How can he want to remain an amateur when he's so clearly superior to his competition? And how can he resist the $10 million or so in endorsement income that is expected to be his as soon as he declares himself a pro?... Jack Nicklaus was a junior when he faced a similar decision in 1961 after winning his only NCAA title.... Nicklaus turned pro in January '62 and won his first U.S. Open that same year....

In the 35 years since Nicklaus's title, the NCAA has been won by such notable future pros as Hale Irwin, Ben Crenshaw, Tom Kite and Phil Mickelson. Only now has the tournament produced a player—and a nickname—who merits comparisons to the young Bear. On the golf course Tiger is that good. But he's also a serious student. "Of the six kids he hangs around with, Tiger says he's the dumbest one," says Kutilda. That's no disgrace. One of his pals is a math whiz who had already passed all of Stanford's basic math courses when he enrolled as a freshman. Another assembled a computer from parts so expertly that it worked from the moment he turned it on. And so on.

As for Woods, he's majoring in economics while trying to prove himself the best collegiate golfer in the nation. Last week he aced the Honors Course.

WHAT NOW?

The talk about Tiger Woods's future continued as he played in his first U.S. Open and another quarter was heard from on the subject—the professionals themselves, many of whom were making decidedly skeptical noises about the phenom's professional future. Good amateur golfer, they sniffed. Woods himself didn't help matters by falling apart over the final five holes of his opening round at Oakland Hills. *BY MICHAEL BAMBERGER*

TOURING PROFESSIONALS DON'T assess Tiger Woods's golf game the way you might. You are awed by the speed of his hands through the ball and the distance he gets with his driver. Touring professionals, in the privacy of their courtesy-car conversations, take a more cold-blooded view. They say, Good amateur golfer.

They know, to paraphrase Bobby Jones, that there is golf and there is professional golf—and they are not at all the same. Scott Verplank was a good amateur who won a Tour event while in college and has been ordinary as a professional. Phil Mickelson was a good amateur who won a Tour event while in college and has been spectacular as a professional. Tiger Woods is a sophomore at Stanford.... He's a superb amateur golfer. But professional golfers will tell you: Everything changes when you start playing for money.

For the first two rounds at the national championship, the USGA sends off the U.S. Amateur, U.S. Open and British Open champs as a threesome, which meant that last Thursday at 12:20 p.m., and again the following morning at 8, Woods, Corey Pavin and John Daly were to be found on the 1st tee at Oakland Hills. Woods, who won the U.S. Amateur last year and the year before, was playing with two of the best professionals in the game.

And, for a while, outplaying them. Through 13 holes in the opening round, Pavin was three over par, Daly was level and Woods was three under. Woods was tied for the lead of the tournament. The gallery following the three was

Even the easygoing Woods couldn't mask his frustration when disaster struck in the first round.

immense from the start, but as word of Woods's round spread across the course, the gallery started to bulge uncomfortably into the wet, malodorous rough. Nobody seemed to mind. The spectators were virtually all white, and they cheered for Woods, who is not, with such verve you had the feeling that maybe American golf is finally emerging from its racist past.

On his way to the 14th tee, Woods sneaked a peak at a leader board and saw he was tied for first. On opening day that should be meaningless, and maybe someday for Woods it will be. On this day it was not. Woods closed like the guy you can beat Sunday morning: bogey, double bogey, quadruple bogey, bogey, bogey.

On a day when his A game was on, Woods shot 76, six over par. On a day when their games were dull, Daly shot 72, Pavin 73.

When the round was over, Woods, the first amateur golfer to have stature on the national sportscape since Jack Nicklaus, put on a brave face and chatted pleasantly with NBC's Johnny Miller in front of a TV camera. A half hour later he was standing by the open trunk of his courtesy car. Wordlessly, he tossed a putter against a golf instruction book, smashed the trunk closed, folded his lanky frame behind the wheel while his father, Earl, took the passenger seat, and got off campus fast.

Daly's been there. "Those things happen," he said sympathetically of Woods's collapse.

"It's happened to me a hundred times. He was going along so well. But he's tough. I wish I was that tough at 21. Hell, I was getting drunk every night when I was 21."

Actually, Woods won't turn 21 until December 30. Before then he's planning to play in two Tour events, Quad Cities and Milwaukee, as an amateur. If he wins either event, he said, he will think about turning pro immediately.

Someday he will turn pro, and when he does, he and Daly will be among the longest drivers extant. The tendency is to lump all the long whackers, but their 36 holes together made it clear that Daly and Woods have wholly different methods. Daly is as flexible as Gumby; his backswing is comically long; his downswing is very steep; and his ball seems to float for a day or so until it returns to terra firma. Woods's swing is classic, and his tee shots have, compared with Daly's, more of a stinging, line-drive-drawing quality to them. On fast fairways or into a wind, Woods is longer. Downwind or on soft, wet fairways—at the Open the grass was long and the fairways mushy—Daly is longer, but not by much....

As they move closer to the hole, Daly's edge over Woods becomes more evident. Daly has an extraordinary feel for how a rolling golf ball will respond to humps and hollows and an innate sense of the best way to play a shot. He performs with such looseness and speed you sometimes wonder if he's really trying. With Woods, there's never any doubt. His manner is technical and analytical. His skill level is very high, but skill and talent are not the same thing.

At Augusta in April, and again at the Open, lag putting appeared to be a weakness in Woods's game. Putting from 30 or more feet, Woods often left himself with cranky three- and four-footers. Facing putts of that length every third hole or so makes for a mental drain that even a smart kid like Woods doesn't need.

Woods says he is very happy with his lag putting, even after a second round that included three three-putts. With better putting his laudable 69 for the round could have been even niftier. The problem, he said, was the awkward places his approach shots ended up, not the lag stroke itself.... But Woods is old enough to know that Nicklaus won a bunch of majors reaching par-5s in two shots and coaxing eagle putts close enough to tap in. Daly, with his wristy stroke, does the same thing. He nudges the ball right to the lip.

The normal route to the Tour for the elite amateur is four years of college golf followed by a journey through the hell known as the Tour Q school.... "Qualifying shouldn't be a problem for him," said last year's U.S. Open champion.

Woods's relaxed charm continued to attract king-sized galleries at Oakland Hills.

Note, however, that Mr. Pavin said shouldn't, not won't. The pro golfer knows to take nothing for granted. An amateur may have all sorts of game. Playing for money, things change.

With a 72-69-73-73-287, Daly finished 27th at Oakland Hills, nine strokes behind Steve Jones. Pavin shot 73-70-72-74-289 for 40th place. Tiger Woods had a 76-69-77-72-294. A spectacular amateur career continues, for now.

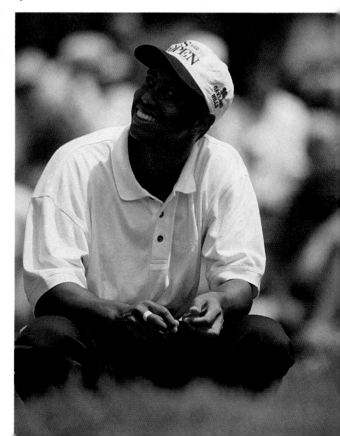

ACT III
THE PRO

ACT III
THE PRO

BY JOHN GARRITY

IT HAS BEEN said that a camel will pass through the eye of a needle before the winner of the Disney World-Magic Kingdom Classic makes the cover of *Sports Illustrated*. Tiger Woods accomplished the latter feat in October 1996, when he won his second Tour event in eight weeks as a pro and then landed, for the first time, smack on *SI*'s glossy face.

Senior writer Rick Reilly covered the Disney for *SI*. Or, rather, he rushed to Orlando when it appeared that Tiger might win. In the office vernacular, it was Reilly's turn to "baby-sit" the kid. Before Reilly, they sent the beanpole writer from Kansas City, the bearded golf writer from Florida, the new guy from Connecticut and *Golf World*, the one-time sports columnist from Boston and the college football expert from Louisville.

"The full editorial resources of the magazine have been thrown at this story," said *SI* golf editor Jim Herre, commanding the Tiger watch from his office in New York. "For the first time since I've been here, the top editors are paying attention to every Tour event. They want to know where Tiger stands, who we've got on the scene, and what the ramifications are if he wins."

With picture-perfect form Woods has stormed the pros, winning twice in his first eight weeks.

IN TWO MONTHS
AS A PRO, HE HAS
TRANSFORMED
AN ENTIRE SPORT

The Disney win landed Tiger on the *SI* cover.

SI's interest was a source of amusement to the PGA Tour's communications staff, who greeted each successive writer/photographer team with a sarcastic, "Welcome to the Tiger Tour." Of course, *SI* wasn't alone on the bandwagon. At some tournaments, media parking lots overflowed and press rooms throbbed with activity. Accredited photographers clutched their red armbands, fearful lest they fall into the hands of some linen-suited Peter Lorre bent on profit or revenge.

Furthermore, for every carpetbagger toting a Powerbook or a telephoto lens, you saw a hundred new golf fans: black teenage boys in baggy shorts and Nikes; Asian grandparents with wisdom wrinkles; young women with tattooed ankles. At the B.C. Open, in Endicott, New York, people outside the grounds held up I NEED TICKETS signs. At the Texas Open, in San Antonio, rock slides were a problem as spectators climbed outcroppings to get a glimpse of Tiger. ("Guys, we're trying to play golf here," Tour veteran David Frost lectured spectators churning behind the 12th tee. "Stand still!")

Earl Woods, standing outside the Texas Open press tent, could only shake his head and issue a warning to players and public alike. "They have no idea what his 'A' game is," Tiger's father said. "They haven't seen it. When Tiger has it, he just *destroys* a golf course."

Back in New York, it was Herre's task to suggest fresh angles on the Woods story and to guide his writers as they sought to place Tiger's bright light where it belonged in the sports spectrum. "I think it's much deeper than simply a young golfer being successful," Herre said. "Tiger transcends that." But Herre didn't want to lose sight of the fact that Woods was still a very young man. Two years before, when he had sat next to Tiger at a college tournament dinner in Hilton Head, South Carolina, Herre had chatted briefly with the 18-year-old—and learned little. "I got a bigger kick out of just listening to him talk with the other kids," Herre said. "School. Golf courses. What they planned to do after graduation. It's a whole different persona when he's with his peers—more relaxed, more open. His voice even changes."

SI's voice changes, too, when an athlete seems—as Herre put it—"transcendent." Mantle, Ali, Nicklaus, Montana, Gretzky, Jordan—they all achieved icon status in part because *their* best drew the attention of *SI*'s best.

But heed the words of Earl Woods, who claims we have not yet seen Tiger at his best.

"Frightening," the father says with transcendent glee. "It will be frightening."

How transcendent? Woods scored his first ace as a pro in his first event, the Milwaukee Open.

ROARING AHEAD

By the time that Tiger Woods had won his third U.S. Amateur in typically heart-stopping fashion, the word was out. On the following Wednesday, he would make the announcement that golfing experts had been expecting for six months: He was leaving Stanford to enter the professional ranks. How would Tiger fare as a pro? If his performance at Pumpkin Ridge was any indication, Tiger's future would be just fine. *BY JAIME DIAZ*

LONG ODDS ARE still available on Tiger Woods's achieving his goal of becoming the greatest golfer of all time. But after the breathtaking way in which he made history by winning the most dramatic U.S. Amateur ever, would a wise man bet against him?

Even with his unprecedented three consecutive victories in the Amateur—the latest attained in a heart-stopping 38th-hole win at Pumpkin Ridge near Portland over an unyielding Steve Scott—the 20-year-old Woods is a long way from making a serious dent in the record of Jack Nicklaus, who has won 18 professional majors along with two Amateurs. But not even Nicklaus's career got off to a better start and, Lord, does Woods know how to finish.

He has been winning national champi-onships since he was 15, when he won the first of his three straight U.S. Junior titles. Now, after six consecutive years as a USGA champion, Woods has achieved the closure that will allow him to join Bobby Jones and Nicklaus in the record book as the greatest amateurs ever, while at the same time ending the debate over whether he should turn pro.... Woods, who is the NCAA champion, will withdraw from Stanford on the eve of what would have been his junior year, with a promise to his parents that he will return to complete his degree sometime in the future.

Woods's immediate plans are ambitious: He wants to qualify for the 1997 PGA Tour by earning enough money in the next two months to get himself into the top 125 on this year's

An early-morning practice session kept Tiger's swing well-grooved for the 36-hole final.

money list. His passport will be the seven sponsors' exemptions annually allowed a player. After Milwaukee, Woods plans to play in the Canadian Open, the Quad City Classic, the B.C. Open, the Las Vegas Invitational, the Texas Open and the Disney/Oldsmobile Classic. If he wins a tournament, Woods will be exempt from having to qualify for two years; if he earns more than $150,000 over the remainder of the year, he should make the top 125. Should he fall short, he will have to qualify for the '97 Tour by earning one of the 40 or so spots available at the dread PGA Tour Qualifying Tournament....

Woods had been seriously thinking about turning pro since a wondrous 66 in the second round of July's British Open. "Something really clicked that day, like I had found a whole new style of playing," he said on Sunday. "I finally understood the meaning of playing within myself. Ever since, the game has seemed a lot easier."

[After the final] Woods, too drained from the week's 164 holes of competition for anything but pizza and a shower at the Portland home where he was staying, explained his decision. "I had intended to stay in school, play four years at Stanford and get my degree, but things change," he said. "I didn't know my game was going to progress to this point. It got harder to get motivated for college matches, and since I accomplished my goal of winning the NCAA, it

was going to get harder still. Finally, winning the third Amateur in a row is a great way to go out. I always said I would know when it was time, and now is the time...."

When Woods's father, Earl, saw that his son was serious about turning pro, he had opened the most high-powered bidding war ever for a golfer. A source close to Woods says that Woods's endorsement deals with Nike (shoes and clothes) and Titleist (ball and clubs) will add up to at least $37 million over the next five years....

[Winning his third U.S. Amateur] was no small task after he stumbled badly, going 4 down in the opening nine of the 36-hole final against Scott, a pugnacious 19-year-old who this week began his sophomore year at Florida. Nearly 15,000 fans—the biggest gallery at an Amateur since Jones chased down the Grand Slam at Merion in Philadelphia in 1930—saw Woods relentlessly fight back from what grew into a five-hole deficit with 16 to play. In doing so, Woods was reprising his comeback from the same margin with 13 holes left in the '94 Amateur final against Trip Kuehne....

Woods hit 28 of the last 29 greens in regulation. During the afternoon 18, when Scott shot what would have been a solid two-under-par 70 in medal play, Woods caught him with a bogeyless 65, the low round in a championship that had begun seven days earlier with 312 competitors. Tellingly, so focused was Woods on his prey that he had no idea until after the match that his score had been so low. "Given the circumstances," he said, "this has to be the best I've ever played."

Woods rallied by winning three straight holes beginning on the 21st. He closed to within a hole, but then Scott sank a spectacular flop shot on the 28th to go 2 up. Woods got the momentum back on the next hole, a 553-yard par-5, when he hit a 350-yard drive and a five-iron to within 45 feet of the cup and rolled in a curling downhill putt for an eagle that trumped Scott's birdie. Scott again answered with a birdie on the 32nd, where Woods missed a six-footer to halve.

Two down with three left, Woods holed an eight-footer for a winning birdie on the 34th hole. Then on the 35th he put aside his frustration at pushing his approach 35 feet from the pin, narrowed his focus and drained his putt. "That's a feeling I'll remember for the rest of my life," said Woods, who repeatedly uppercut the air after his ball had dropped.

The rivals halved the 36th hole, and on the first hole of sudden death, Scott missed an 18-footer for the championship. Finally, on the 38th hole, the 194-yard, par-3 10th, Woods hit a softly fading six-iron, a shot he and Harmon have been working to perfect for more than a

Woods left no doubt about his emotions after sinking the tying 35-footer on the 35th hole.

year, to 12 feet. Scott pushed his five-iron into the greenside rough and chipped 11 feet past the pin. Woods missed his putt, but so did Scott, and when Woods drilled an 18-incher into the hole to take the lead for the first time, the championship was over....

Now Woods has a new pro career ahead and a new set of goals. If he gets off to a good start and keeps coming through with the fast finishes that made him an amateur for the ages, perhaps the odds on catching Nicklaus will grow shorter.

ON THE JOB TRAINING

Needless to say, when Tiger Woods made his debut as a professional at the Milwaukee Open just four days after his triumph at the U.S. Amateur, the public interest was intense. Leigh Montville was on hand to report on the hysteria surrounding the young star and to chart the progress of golf's newest savior. *BY LEIGH MONTVILLE*

THE KID WOULD escape from inside Tiger Woods every now and then, the way a five-year-old will come downstairs in pajamas and announce to the adult gathering in the living room that he can't sleep. A smile would come across his face in just a certain way. A phrase would escape from his lips. A nice little laugh.

"I got a courtesy car," he would say, amazed at the fact. "I still can't rent a car, but they gave me a courtesy car."

"I got all these clothes delivered Wednesday, yes, but the best thing was they came in these great bags," he would say. "They're unbelievable bags. They have all these pockets and stuff. Just the best."

The adult would come back into control soon enough—the bright and earnest young man on his first week on the job as the multi-millionaire Savior of Golf and Unifier of All Peoples—but the glimpses of the kid were the best part. Underneath that composed, articulate, talented, marketable *commodity* who was competing in the Greater Milwaukee Open, there was a 20-year-old human being off on a grand adventure. He was playing his game on the stage where he had always wanted to play it.

"It was great just to get back to what I do, play golf," he said after firing a 67 in his first round as a professional, on the way to making the cut and finishing tied for 60th with a seven-under-par 277 and receiving a paycheck of $2,544. "That's what I know best. That's what I've always done."

Signed last week to endorsement contracts that might be worth more than $60 million—the estimates getting higher and wackier with

Woods overcame a shaky third round to post a solid performance in his first pro tournament.

each passing day—and introduced to the country with a blitzkrieg of weekend advertising by Nike, Woods was trapped in probably the most publicized debut in American sporting history. What was bigger? Every day suggestions were made in the press room. David Clyde, teenager, pitching for the Texas Rangers? Jim Craig playing goal for the Atlanta Flames after the Olympics? Gretzky? Wilt? Eric Lindros? Jennifer Capriati? What? The Beatles at Shea Stadium?...

Woods was clearly the most heralded golf prodigy since ... who? Nicklaus? He already hits the ball farther than almost anyone else on the Tour and has been dealing with pressure since the start of his teens. With his multiracial heritage (African-American, Thai, a touch of American Indian and Caucasian) he is the perfect picture for the natural-fibers future of a game that has forever been mostly white and Ban-Lon.

Who can he be? Pick a name. Arthur Ashe. Jackie Robinson. Colin Powell. A male Naomi Campbell. Darius Rucker, singing with those Blowfish. Any of the above. All of the above. All he has to do is scorch a few golf courses, win a few majors, become the best player in the entire world. That's all. Starting now.

Tiger read the greens well but may have used up his quota of dramatic putts at the Amateur.

"He's come along at exactly the right time," says Loren Roberts, who won the $1.2 million tournament in a playoff with Jerry Kelly. "He's like Arnold Palmer, a guy who is going to popularize the sport to a bigger audience, to reach out to areas where maybe golf has been slow to reach. He's got a lot on his shoulders. There's no question he's going to do well. When you hit your best shot and look up and he's 60 yards in front of you, that's impressive, to start. But he's still going to have to beat those 156 other guys out here. That's not going to be as easy as some people think...."

For most of the four tournament days—well, for all of the days until he finished early on Sunday and attention could be turned to the leaders—Woods was the headline performer, with no one a close second. All of the other galleries from the record GMO crowds on the course, added together, wouldn't have equaled the size of his. "It didn't bother me," Woods said. "I'm used to it. Besides, if you lose a ball, there are a lot of people out there to help you find it."

Losing balls was not a problem last Thursday and Friday. He was still feeding off momentum from the Amateur, and both his first-day 67 and second-day 69 could have been lower if he had made some putts. ("I think I used them up in the Amateur," he said.) His first shot as a pro, let it be noted, was a 336-yard drive straight down the middle. He later described it as his most memorable shot of the tournament.

On the third day the momentum turned to fatigue. Woods found trouble and scrambled for his 73, which effectively knocked him out of a high finish.... He was back in form for the final day, when he shot 68 and made a hole in one—the ninth of his life—on the 188-yard 14th.

"I played with him on his bad day, nothing working for him, and I was impressed," said veteran Bruce Lietzke. "You learn about somebody when he's having that kind of day. A lot of 20-year-olds would get frustrated, angry. He never lost his temper, still kept working. If he's going to be the game's next great ambassador, then the game is in good hands...."

After finishing on Sunday, [Woods] was on his way to the next Tour stop, the Canadian Open, outside Toronto. "What would you be doing if you hadn't dropped out of Stanford and turned pro?" a reporter asked. "Would you be registering now for classes?"

"No, school doesn't start until September 25," the kid said, sneaking out for a moment. "And you don't have to register. The student body is so small that you can just go to classes, find ones you like, then sign up for them. I went 3½ weeks one semester trying a lot of them before I finally registered."

Ah, but none of that now. Back to work. This new and different school was in session, and the tests had only just begun.

NO PAIN, NO GAIN

In his third pro start, Tiger Woods appeared ready to take another step in his already fabled career by winning a PGA event. But the final day brought some hard lessons for Woods as he saw his lead swept away by a most atypical collapse.   *BY JAIME DIAZ*

TIGER WOODS HAS spoiled us. Five months ago he said his goals were to win the NCAA Championship and an unprecedented third straight U.S. Amateur, and he accomplished both. After turning pro, he said he aimed to win enough money in only seven tournaments to secure his PGA Tour card. At first we were dubious, but then he played with such power and poise that his plan seemed more modest than unreasonable. Now when he says he intends to win a Tour event, as he did last week on the eve of the Quad City Classic in Coal Valley, Illinois, we take him at his word. So when Woods shot a second-round 64 that included six straight birdies to take the lead at Oakwood Country Club and held steady with a third-round 67, a good portion of the golf world, and almost all the other people who don't care about the game

but are crazy about Tiger, believed the 20-year-old would take another giant step.

There were some valid statistical reasons to bank on Woods on Sunday, such as the eye-popping 312.5-yard driving average and the gaudy 68.5 stroke average from his first 10 rounds as a pro. But mostly that belief was based on empirical evidence. Woods has demonstrated a genius for getting the job done, closing the deal. "Let the legend grow"—the seductive mantra of his father, who has never been surprised by his son's accomplishments—has become a subliminal battle cry for Tiger. But in Sunday's final round, the game answered back. Golf inflicts pain on those who play it, and there are no exceptions. Ben Crenshaw and Jack Nicklaus, whose early careers parallel Woods's, absorbed a Tour bagful of psychic harpoons early on,

Though Woods struggled in the fourth round, he still finished a more-than-respectable fifth.

with Nicklaus's tough hide proving an indispensible part of his greatness. Woods might be made of similar stuff, but the definitive tests have yet to be conducted. Sunday's ordeal (he closed with a two-over-par 72 to finish tied for fifth at eight under, four strokes behind winner Ed Fiori) can be considered his first pop quiz.

On Sunday, Woods found himself in unknown territory. His young man's propensity for making the big number, plus an alarming inability to steady a jumpy putter, cost him a tournament he knows he could have won with even an average performance. As Woods licked his wounds, the legend went into remission. After starting the day with a 337-yard drive down the middle of the 1st fairway, Woods birdied the second hole, and as he stood on the 4th tee, he saw his name atop the leader board with a three-stroke lead over such unimposing pros as Jay Delsing, Phil Blackmar and Fiori, with whom he was paired. But playing for a fade off the tee on the 460-yard 4th, a hole that doglegs to the right, Woods rushed his downswing and hit a double cross he's likely to remember. His ball flew left over trees and into a pond. As Woods said later, "From there, the adventure began."

A visit to the heavy rough on a steep embankment was just one stop on Tiger's fearsome 4th.

Woods had to take a penalty drop on a steep embankment in heavy rough that left him the option of chipping back to the fairway or trying to reach the green, some 200 yards away, by blasting an iron through an opening in the trees that was about the size of a doorway. He chose poorly, deciding to go for the green. Woods pushed his six-iron shot, and the ball caromed dead left off an oak limb, disappearing into the bright green algae of the hazard. Another penalty, a chip out, an approach and two putts later, Woods had completed a quadruple-bogey 8.

Trailing by a stroke and suddenly looking very young, Woods rallied to par the 5th and birdie the par-5 6th. But when it appeared that he might be summoning a comeback of U.S. Amateur proportions, Woods somehow four-jacked the relatively flat 7th green from the astonishing distance of eight feet. Woods pulled his birdie try four feet by, jabbed the comebacker the same distance in the other direction and barely grazed the left lip with his third putt. He finally sank a three-footer for double-bogey 6. Quad City, indeed.

The wreck was more shocking than the nine strokes Woods lost to par over the final five holes of the opening round at the U.S. Open at Oakland Hills, after he was tied for the lead. "I was shocked," said Earl Woods, finally admitting surprise. "I thought that reaction would be all over with after the U.S. Open. But that was a first round. This was a final round. It's a new, valuable lesson."

Playing through his disappointment, Woods dug deep for four more birdies that salvaged a tie for fifth, but a golden opportunity had slipped away. Woods was the only player among the top 18 finishers to shoot higher than 69 on Sunday. At crunch time he had been crunched by a field weakened by the Presidents Cup....

In 14 years Woods might look back fondly on the Quad City Classic. He did many things well. On a day in which he had two penalty strokes and a four-putt, he battled back with six birdies to finish with a respectable score. In righting himself when all hope of victory was lost, he did the professional thing, winning a nice check. He has four tournaments to avoid a trip to Q school, where the hurt can be permanent.

"I see progress," Woods says. "I keep getting better. It's hard to say right now what I learned. I'll know better in a couple of days. I will tell you one thing: I will learn a lot from this."

He knows now. Quad City was perhaps the first real setback in Woods's heretofore charmed career.... The foremost lesson might be one that will be reinforced over and over in the years to come: no pain, no gain.

CROWD PLEASER

Jaime Diaz spent some time with Tiger Woods both before and during the B.C. Open and returned with this report on a week in the life of a budding superstar. For the record, Woods's third-place finish represented his best pro performance to date. *BY JAIME DIAZ*

IF HE WEREN'T someone who carries out his missions like a Saturday-morning action hero, Tiger Woods could have been expected to hit the wall at last week's B.C. Open. The B.C. is the PGA Tour at its least glamorous. The tournament is played in Endicott, a suburb of economically depressed Binghamton in upstate New York, at En-Joie Golf Club, an austere public track high on hospitality but low on ambience. "Life looks hard around here," said Woods after cruising around town in the Ford Explorer provided by the tournament.

Woods came to Endicott overgolfed and nearly overwhelmed by his burgeoning celebrity. Counting the U.S. Amateur, in which he played 164 holes in six days, Woods was beginning his fifth straight week of competition. His most recent outing had been a demoralizing tie for fifth at the Quad City Classic in Coal Valley, Illinois, where he lost a three-stroke lead in the final round. In addition to the self-induced pressure of trying to earn his Tour card, Woods has had to contend with a crush of interviews, book deals, business propositions and autograph seekers....

MONDAY: Woods has a way of turning negatives into positives. The final-round debacle at Quad City was put into a healthy perspective at a Sunday-night dinner with his father, Earl, swing coach Butch Harmon, manager Hughes Norton, and best friend Bryon Bell, also 20 and a premed student at UC San Diego. "By dessert we were laughing about how bad I blew it," Woods says. "What I did is part of a learning process. I've done it before. If that's my last time, great. But it probably won't be. In golf, you lose more than you win...."

At the B.C. Open, eager crowds pressed to catch a mere glimpse of Woods (white shirt and cap).

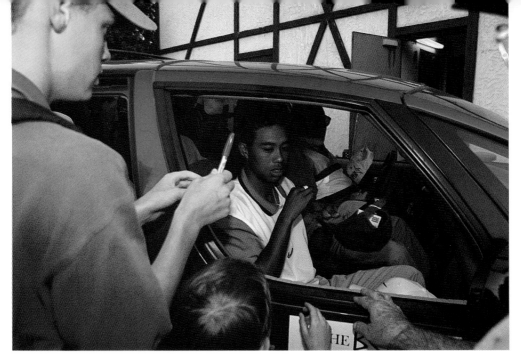

Ever courteous, Woods signed autographs wherever the fans found him.

TUESDAY: In the afternoon Woods and his agents meet with Nike executives, who bring several boxes of apparel. Woods selects some two-tone shirts with block color patterns. The shirts could become part of the Swoosh 18 line Nike is preparing for him. One end of the living room in Woods's suite is strewn with boxes of shirts, slacks, sweaters and shoes, the other with a half-dozen putters that he compulsively uses to stroke balls at table legs.

After the meeting Woods is philosophical. "Sometimes it's hard to remember that I'm calling the shots," he says. "Butch has already told me I have to be strong enough to say no and tell people who are working for me what to do, including him. In a way I've gone from being a college sophomore to a mini-CEO. It's kind of hard. I mean, I'm 20 years old…."

WEDNESDAY: Norton [leaves Binghamton but] will return on Sunday to accompany Woods to Orlando, where he will finally get a look at his new house, a villa at Isleworth where his neighbors are Arnold Palmer, Mark McCormack and

Mark O'Meara as well as Shaquille O'Neal, Ken Griffey Jr. and Wesley Snipes.... Woods confesses that he doesn't really feel like a pro, or rich, despite the reported $60 million worth of deals he has struck with Nike and Titleist....

THURSDAY: [Woods] is ready when the bell rings. On his first hole he makes a 10-footer for a birdie. On his 14th hole, the 565-yard, par-5 5th, Woods smashes two drivers into a strong wind to reach the front fringe, but then mishits a six-iron chip and pushes the 12-footer for birdie. Angry, he snaps his fist against his thigh and curses. He birdies the next hole and doesn't mishit a shot the rest of the way. After a 68 that leaves him two strokes off the lead, Woods says, "I got mad back there for a reason. I could feel myself getting complacent, probably because I've been on the road so long. I had to snap out of it and use anger for some energy...."

FRIDAY: On the back nine Woods finishes with an explosion, birdieing the last three holes for a 66. It puts him at eight under, three strokes behind leader Pete Jordan. With a per-round scoring average of just over 68 since turning pro, Woods's game has been difficult to criticize. Distance control with his irons, Woods's bugaboo at the last two Masters, has been exemplary. "Because I'm doing it every day with no distractions from school, my understanding of how to play is increasing," he says. "One of the reasons I wasn't good at Tour events before is I could never get into a rhythm and a flow."

SATURDAY: Woods finishes with another 66 and remains three shots behind the leaders....

SUNDAY: Woods is pleased to feel the drizzle that begins when he birdies the 3rd hole. "I wanted the conditions to be hard because it's easier to catch up," he says. But his mood changes when he sees that Fred Funk has birdied four of the first six holes and is six shots ahead of him. "Guys out here can just go off," he says. "Only a couple of us could do that in college. On Tour, everybody can."

By the time Woods reaches the 7th hole, play is suspended. Two hours later the final round is canceled. Woods ties for third with [Patrick] Burke, yet while packing for his flight to Orlando, he refuses to celebrate. "I'm not there yet," he says. "I feel good because no one thought I would be able to bounce back after last week, but I did. That shows I'm tough enough to deal with disappointment, but it won't mean anything if I don't keep my focus. I've just got to keep going."

JACKPOT!

Finally, the inevitable: In his fifth pro tournament, Tiger Woods notched his first win. In the process he ended all the talk about money lists and Q school and next year's exemptions. He also justified all the comparisons to the greats of the game and proved beyond doubt that a new age—call it the Tiger Era—was dawning in golf. *BY GARY VAN SICKLE*

GOLF, AS WE know it, is over. It came to an end on a chamber-of-commerce Sunday evening in Las Vegas when Tiger Woods went for the upgrade: He's not just a promising young Tour pro anymore, he's an era.

Three straight U.S. Amateur titles and $60 million in endorsements before he laced up his first pair of you-know-whats provided a strong clue, but when Woods shot 64 in the final round of the Las Vegas Invitational and then beat Davis Love III—a big dog on the PGA Tour—on the first hole of a playoff at the TPC at Summerlin, the start of the new age became official. The game's most heralded amateur since Bobby Jones has his maiden pro victory, and nothing is likely to be the same. Woods, at 20, is already the biggest name in the sport.

Why? Because he is as good as he looks. Start with the length. You thought John Daly was long? Woods is longer, and much straighter off the tee. In the light desert air of Las Vegas, the ball travels an extra 10%, but Woods's 323-yard driving average for the week was 13 yards better than that of John Adams, who was second, and 38 yards better than the field's. On Sunday, Woods, going for the green at the short par-4 15th, flew his tee shot into the back bunker, a carry of about 315 yards—with a three-wood.

Jack Nicklaus has long contended that someone would come along who could hit 30 yards past everyone else, much as he did decades ago, have a great short game and dominate the sport. That someone could be Woods. He's a good putter who gets better in the clutch, in

Woods's stunning win had everyone wondering: Is he the dominant player Nicklaus foresaw?

the mold of Nicklaus and Lee Trevino. Whenever Nicklaus had to make a 10- or 20-footer, he did. Woods does, too. He did it on Sunday when he ran in a 30-footer for birdie at the 11th, the key hole of his round. Woods had driven into a fairway bunker and appeared to be in trouble, yet he was able to muscle a sand wedge onto the front of the green, and his long putt never wavered. Watching, you somehow knew the ball was going to drop.

Woods has all the extras, starting with the instantly recognizable nickname. He smiles on the course and looks as if he's having fun. He emotes, whether it's punching the air with an uppercut, last seen at the Amateur, or straight-arming a putt into the hole.

In Las Vegas everything added up to a victory that was part incredible, part inevitable. "We were afraid he was going to win before he got here," said Jim Cook, the tournament director, whose event is now linked forever with the kid....

Woods played like a man among boys during his two years at Stanford and throughout his unparalleled reign as an amateur. So far the Tour hasn't been any different. Exhausted from the 36-hole days at the U.S. Amateur, Woods tied for 60th in his debut in the Greater Milwaukee Open and has improved every week—11th, fifth, third and first—for the fastest start since Michael Johnson....

After a disappointing 70 in the first round [at Summerlin], Woods seemed to have as much chance of winning as Bob Dole. The Tour record for a 72-hole tournament is 27 under par, set by Mike Souchak in 1955. Woods played the last 72 holes of this 90-hole event in 26 under. A second-round 63 got him back in the picture. He followed with 68 and 67 before Sunday's 64.

Woods and Love found it odd that they met in the playoff. They had played a nine-hole practice round at the Buick Challenge the week before, and Woods told Love that it would be cool to go head-to-head down the stretch someday. "When I saw his name on the board, I thought, He got what he wanted," said Love.

Woods, who started the final round in a five-way tie for seventh, is a dangerous golfer. Difficult situations bring out the best in him. He came from 5 down in two of his championship matches in the Amateur. He came from four shots back at Summerlin, and he did it with a limp. Woods aggravated a groin injury, a hangover from the Amateur, during Friday's round at the Desert Inn. On Sunday he grimaced in pain and held his left leg after hitting a hard two-iron from an uphill lie on the 13th fairway....

Despite the victory—which brings a two-year exemption, gets him into next year's Masters and lifts him to 40th on the money

Woods's glitzy companions showed just how far he had traveled from the amateur ranks.

list with $437,194—and the injury, Woods says he will play in this week's Texas Open....

A player like Woods comes along once in a lifetime. He aims high, probably higher than we know. Before Las Vegas, before he got within range of his stated goal of making the top 125 on the money list and earning an exemption for next year, Woods asked Love if he might make the '97 Ryder Cup team if he won three or four times before next August. "He's not playing for the money," Love said on Sunday. "He never thought, I have to make another one hundred and some thousand dollars to make the top 125. He's trying to win. He thinks about winning and nothing else. I like the way he thinks. We were all trying to prolong the inevitable. We knew he was going to win. I just didn't want it to be today. Everybody better watch out: He's going to be a force."

For now, he's just a kid—a very talented kid who after his victory on Sunday was looking forward to returning to Las Vegas in a year, when he'll be 21. "I'll be legal," Woods said, smiling. "I can actually do some stuff around here."

He already has. Golf may never be the same.

TOP CAT

As if the cake needed any icing, Tiger Woods went out two weeks after his first Tour victory and won again, this time at the Disney Classic in Orlando, thereby providing Rick Reilly with an opportunity to examine the many ways in which this prodigiously talented 20-year-old had transformed the very face of golf.   *BY RICK REILLY*

To UNDERSTAND WHAT golf is now, don't watch Tiger Woods. Watch who *watches* Tiger Woods. Young black women in tight jeans and heels. Tour caddies, back out on the course after hauling a bag 18 holes. White arbitrageurs with cell phones. Giant groups of fourth-graders, mimicking their first golf swings. Pasty golf writers who haven't left the press tent since the days of Fat Jack. Hispanic teens in Dallas Cowboys jerseys trying to find their way around a golf course for the first time in their lives. Bus drivers and CEOs and mothers with strollers catching the wheels in the bunkers as they go.

History will do that. History will suck you into places you have never been. Woods is making history almost daily. Last week at Disney World in Orlando, the throngs following him turned every tee box into the line at Space Mountain, and he gave them still more history, winning for a cereal-spoon-dropping second time in his first seven starts—the greatest professional debut in golf history—and bankrolling his way to 23rd on the Tour's money list and the pole position in this week's gaudy Tour Championship at Southern Hills in Tulsa. The way things were supposed to work, Tiger was to tee it up at the PGA Tour Qualifying Tournament in December to try to earn his card. He even sent in the $3,000 entry fee. He can void the check now. From Tour school to Tour Championship in seven weeks. The kid's a quick study.

They will show up in Tulsa, too, this tsunami of Tiger Tailers, dipping their big toes into the game for the first time, hoping to answer the question, Is this really happening?... For his

Woods's vision was 20-20 in Orlando where he beat a rejuvenated Stewart for his second victory.

WALT DISNEY WORLD / OLDSMOBILE
GOLF CLASSIC

| T. WOODS | 2 | 2 |
| P. STEWART | 2 | 0 |

seven-week scorched-divot tour since he became a professional on August 28, tournament directors conservatively estimate that he has drawn an extra 150,000 fans. And this is not Chicago and Los Angeles. This is Coal Valley, Illinois, and Endicott, New York. No wonder that when Woods committed to play the Disney, the tournament director jumped into a swimming pool.

Whoo-boy. Maybe those Nike ads had it right. Is golf ready for this? Golf used to be four white guys sitting around a pinochle table talking about their shaft flexes and deciding whether to have the wilted lettuce soup. Now golf is Cindy Crawford sending Woods a letter. A youngster who'd been promised a round of golf with Woods was bouncing all around his Orlando home two weeks ago, going, "When is Tiger coming? When is Tiger coming?" The kid's name? Ken Griffey Jr....

When was the last time a 20-year-old showed up and grabbed an entire sport by the throat? The Disney was Woods's fifth straight top-five finish. Not only has no rookie ever come within a moon shot of doing that, but also no *player* has done it since Curtis Strange 14 years ago....

With a spring-loaded bomb of a swing [Woods] may make the term *par 5* obsolete. For Woods there *are* no par-5s. At the 595-yard

14th on Saturday at Disney's Magnolia Course, Woods still had 284 yards to go over trees and a green-guarding lake. He cold starched a three-wood—over the green. In his seven starts he has birdied 68 of the 128 par-5s he has played, including 12 of 16 at the Disney.

It has been a kind of blister bliss for Woods's caddie, Mike (Fluff) Cowan, who is having to pace off ponds and trees and Häagen-Dazs stands that until now have never been in play in his 20 years on the Tour. Last week Fluff may have become the first caddie in history to utter this sentence: "It's 290 to clear that bunker. I like three-wood."...

What's so charming about this historic ride is the tournaments where it has all played out—Milwaukee, Quad City, the Texas Open, B.C.—the end-of-the-year-liquidation-sale events that nobody enters unless he's hurting for his card or took a wrong turn at Doral. But for this one magic stretch, these places were the Rainbow Rooms.... Still, it's not as if Woods beat nothing but club pros on the Tiger Tour. Of the Top 20 players on the Sony World Ranking, he has beaten Ernie Els (No. 3), Fred Couples (5), Corey Pavin (8) twice, Phil Mickelson (9), Davis Love III (10) twice, Mark O'Meara (11), Vijay Singh (16), Loren Roberts (17), David Duval (19) and Scott Hoch (20)

What pressure? Woods handled the crowds and the competition with his usual grace.

twice. On Sunday at the Disney he matched a rejuvenated Payne Stewart, who needed to win to make Tulsa, birdie for birdie. Woods did him one better, firing a 66 to Stewart's 67 to win....

But it's *how* [Woods] wins that's eerie.... Last Friday morning, as he was having his cereal with his father, he put down the sports pages and made an announcement. "Pop," he said. "Got to shoot 63 today. That's what it will take to get into it."

"So, go do it," droned Earl, half awake.

The little condo they share in Orlando does not get the Golf Channel, the only network that showed the Disney, so Earl heard nothing more about the tournament until that afternoon when his son got home from his new job. "Whaddya shoot?" said Pop, blandly.

"Sixty-three," said Sonny.

"Oh, my god," said Pop.

Hey, aren't kids *supposed* to have fun at Disney World?...

Woods is finding positives all around him, like in the new, throbbing gallery he is inventing: school teachers and Little League teams and whole black families, ... the kind of family that golf never saw except waiting outside the caddie tent....

Listen to how new the sounds are too.

"You go, T!" a young black man yelled at Woods on Sunday. "Take care of *bizness*!"

There was this from two teenage African-American girls—a sight seldom seen in pre-Woodsian golf—just after Tiger had ripped a shot that sounded like a Scud taking off.

"And that ain't *nothin'* yet!" one said.

As Woods passed, they smiled at him and he smiled back.

"Lorrrrrd!" said the other. "He is just *too* cute!"

Woods seems as charged by the voltage from his enormous crowds as everybody else. He will high-five kids, look fans in the eye and actually respond "Thanks" when they holler out, "Kill 'em, Tiger!"... Woods doesn't have Fluff hand out unwanted balls at the end of a round; Woods throws them to kids while he's playing. "I remember when I was a kid, I always wanted to be a part of it," Woods says. "I always wanted to be connected somehow."

Who doesn't? At the Disney a young black man was wandering around with his buddies trying to follow Woods but looking lost. Finally he discreetly approached a black cameraman. "Brother," he said, "can I ask you something?"

The cameraman leaned over the ropes to hear him. "Sure."

"Well," the young man said, "what do we *do*?" He'll have an entire era to learn.

Fluff found himself making some unusual course measurements for golf's newest top banana.

Photo Credits

Cover
Jacqueline Duvoisin

Back Cover
Bob Martin

Introduction
5, John Biever; 6, George Rose; 7, V.J. Lovero; 9, Bob Martin.

Act I: The Kid
10-11, Robert Beck; 13, Robert Beck; 14, V.J. Lovero; 16, Robert Beck; 19, Robert Beck; 21, Robert Walker/USGA; 22, Michael O'Bryon; 24, Michael O'Bryon; 27, Anton Wont/Allsport.

Act II: The Amateur
28-29, John Burgess; 31, Ken Geiger; 32, Bob Martin; 35, Anton Wont/Allsport; 36, V.J. Lovero; 38, Anton Wont/Allsport; 41, Peter Read Miller; 42, Jacqueline Duvoisin; 45, Jacqueline Duvoisin; 46-47, Jacqueline Duvoisin; 49, John Biever; 51, Jacqueline Duvoisin; 53, Jacqueline Duvoisin; 54, Bob Martin; 57, Patrick Murphy-Racey; 58, Patrick Murphy-Racey; 61, John Biever; 63, John Biever.

Act III: The Pro
64-65, Jacqueline Duvoisin; 67, Joe Picciolo; 68, David Walberg; 69, Joe Picciolo; 71, Robert Beck; 73, Robert Beck; 75, John Biever; 76, John Biever; 78, David Walberg; 80, David Walberg; 83, Jacqueline Duvoisin; 84, Jacqueline Duvoisin; 86, Robert Beck; 89, Robert Beck; 90, Jim Gund; 92, Jim Gund; 95, Ben Van Hook.

EPILOGUE

After his victory in the Disney Classic, Tiger Woods appeared in one more PGA tournament in 1996—the Tour Championship at Southern Hills Country Club in Tulsa. The night after Tiger's solid opening round of 70, his father, Earl, was hospitalized with chest pains, leading Tiger to remain at his bedside until after 5 a.m. Exhausted and anxious about his father's health, Woods shot a 78 on Friday, his worst round as a pro. But with Earl much improved and with a good night's rest bolstering him on Saturday, Woods recovered with a 72 and followed that with a 68 on Sunday to finish tied for 21st place. His earnings of $55,800 gave him a total of $790,594 in only eight tournaments as a pro and placed him 25th on the overall Tour money list for 1996.